Issues in Action

GUN VIOLENCE AND THE FIGHT FOR PUBLIC SAFETY

Elliott Smith

Cicely Lewis, Executive Editor

Lerner Publications ◆ Minneapolis

LETTER FROM CICELY LEWIS

Dear Reader,

I started the Read Woke challenge in response to the needs of my students. I wanted my students to read books that challenged social norms, gave voice to the voiceless, and sought to challenge the status quo. Have you ever felt as if the truth was being hidden from you? Have

Cicely Lewis

you ever felt like adults are not telling you the full story because you are too young? Well, I believe you have a right to know about the issues that are plaguing our society. I believe that you have a right to hear the truth.

I created Read Woke Books because I want you to be knowledgeable and compassionate citizens. You will be the leaders of our society soon, and you need to be equipped with knowledge so that you can treat others with the dignity and respect they deserve. And so you can be treated with that same respect.

As you turn these pages, learn about how history has impacted the things we do today. Hopefully you can be the change that helps to make our world a better place for all.

—Cicely Lewis, Executive Editor

TABLE OF CONTENTS

VOICES FOR CHANGE 4

CHAPTER 1
NATIONAL PLAGUE **7**

CHAPTER 2
POLITICAL BATTLE **11**

CHAPTER 3
SOCIETY AND VIOLENCE **16**

CHAPTER 4
A SAFER AMERICA **19**

TAKE ACTION 24
TIMELINE 26
GLOSSARY 28
SOURCE NOTES 29
READ WOKE READING LIST 30
INDEX 31

The Youth Over Guns
March in New York in 2018

VOICES FOR CHANGE

EVERY YEAR IN EARLY JUNE, THOUSANDS OF PEOPLE ACROSS THE UNITED STATES WEAR ORANGE. They march and protest to call attention to gun violence in the US. National Gun Violence Awareness Day is the first Friday in June. And the color orange has become linked to the gun violence prevention movement.

Shortly after performing with her marching band at President Barack Obama's inauguration in 2013, fifteen-year-old Hadiya

Pendleton was killed by a stray bullet. Her friends began to wear orange in her honor. "[It's] the color hunters wear . . . to say 'Don't shoot me,'" one friend explained. The Wear Orange movement has grown ever since.

In 2019 hundreds marched across the Brooklyn Bridge in New York. In Washington, DC, the National Cathedral rang church bells for those killed daily by gun violence. In Los Angeles, celebrities joined calls against gun violence. Virtual events were organized in 2020 to discuss gun violence and police brutality. "I think she would be really proud of us," Hadiya's father, Nate Pendleton, said.

Young activists such as Aalayah Eastmond (*far left*) and Ramon Contreras (*second from left*) organized and attended the 2018 Youth Over Guns March.

In many ways, young people are driving the push to end gun violence. Students Demand Action is a youth-led organization that advocates for commonsense gun reform. Created in 2018, it has more than two hundred chapters in the US. The March for Our Lives group organized the 2018 March for Our Lives rally in Washington, DC. More than two hundred thousand people attended the protest, which featured student speakers. Many of the speakers were survivors of school shootings. They vowed to make changes to US gun laws.

"We will take action every day in every way until they simply cannot ignore us anymore," said Parkland, Florida, shooting survivor and high school student Delaney Tarr.

The 2018 March for Our Lives rally in Washington, DC

Guns can be bought easily in many US stores.

CHAPTER 1
NATIONAL PLAGUE

IN 2019 AN AVERAGE OF 109 PEOPLE PER DAY DIED BY GUN VIOLENCE IN THE US. Many others are seriously injured by guns. The impact of seeing gun violence, or even losing a loved one, can lead to ongoing trauma. People in some communities live in fear of gun violence.

This problem is uniquely American. Per million people per year, the US has six times as many gun-related homicides as Canada has. It has almost sixteen times more than Germany has. The primary reason is that the US has more guns than any other country has. A 2018 report found that combined, Americans own almost four hundred million guns. The US

In open carry states such as Texas, people are allowed to wear weapons where others can see them.

population is 330 million. So, there are more guns than people in the US. It is the only country for which this is true.

Why do Americans have so many guns? The answer is complicated. Many Americans link guns to patriotism, power, and personal safety. The American gun industry continues to thrive. The country has more than twelve thousand gun manufacturers and about fifty-six thousand licensed gun sellers.

Studies show that states with more guns have more gun-related violence and deaths. More than 40 percent of adults own guns in Mississippi, the state with the highest gun death rate in 2018. In Rhode Island, the state with the lowest gun death rate that year, less than 10 percent of adults own guns.

FINDING SOLUTIONS

While the US deals with a serious gun violence issue, other countries have taken steps to reduce guns' impact. New Zealand banned semiautomatic weapons after a terrorist attack in 2019. In 1996 Australia bought over six hundred thousand guns from its citizens and then destroyed them. In Japan, people must pass a series of tough tests before they can own a gun.

Despite pressure from activists, the US federal government has been hesitant to enact new gun laws.

In 2012 President Barack Obama announced that his vice president, Joe Biden (*left*), would lead a national effort to slow gun violence.

A mass shooting is one in which four or more people are injured or killed by someone using a firearm. In the US, mass shootings occur at least once a day.

"No other developed nation tolerates the level of gun violence that we do," Obama wrote in a 2019 statement. "We are not helpless here. And until all of us stand up and insist on holding public officials accountable for changing our gun laws, these tragedies will keep happening."

Pro-Second Amendment protesters stand outside the New Mexico State Capitol in 2020.

CHAPTER 2
POLITICAL BATTLE

MANY UNDERSTAND THE SECOND AMENDMENT OF THE US CONSTITUTION AS PROTECTING ANY AMERICAN'S RIGHT TO KEEP AND BEAR ANY KIND OF GUN. This constitutional right forms the backbone of many progun arguments. But the Second Amendment was passed in 1791. It spoke specifically of a well-regulated militia, an armed group called to serve as soldiers only in emergencies. Most modern gun owners do not belong to militias as the Founding Fathers would have understood them. The US was very different then. So were the weapons Americans had at their disposal.

A modern semiautomatic rifle above a rifle from 1894

Modern guns are much more powerful than weapons were over two hundred years ago. Then guns fired far fewer rounds, fired much more slowly, and took a long time to reload. Some modern guns, such as automatic weapons, fire many times with a single press of the trigger. These weapons are found in many American homes. Private citizens have amassed arsenals. Nearly half the guns in the US are owned by 3 percent of American adults. Progun advocates use the concepts of freedom and liberty to explain why someone may want to own multiple guns. But the Second Amendment doesn't necessarily guarantee the right to carry military-grade weapons on the street.

In 2008 the Supreme Court ruled for the first time that individuals could have guns for personal uses such as self-defense. Since then, policies across the US have made it easier to acquire and carry guns.

The National Rifle Association, a gun advocacy group, has played a major role in the battle to define the Second Amendment. The group has argued that the right to own a

REFLECT

Do you believe everyone has the right to own a gun? Why or why not?

National Rifle Association merchandise on display at an Iowa political event in 2011

> ## "In my viewpoint, it is not necessary to rewrite the Second Amendment in order to get to a world with fewer guns."
>
> **—Igor Volsky, founder of Guns Down America, a nonprofit advocacy group**

gun is an individual issue similar to free speech or religion and should not be regulated by the government. The organization has spent more than $50 million since 1998 to lobby politicians to pass progun laws. It has also spent

The so-called gun show loophole allows buyers to purchase guns from certain sellers at shows without passing a background check. Progun politicians rarely act to close this kind of loophole.

President Trump often spoke at campaign rallies of his strong support for Second Amendment rights.

millions in campaign donations to support candidates who favor fewer gun laws.

Some use the Second Amendment to support their viewpoint. To rally his supporters, President Donald Trump often claimed that Democrats would take individuals' guns away. Democrats said they wanted to strengthen gun laws to cut down on gun violence.

Often gun violence has multiple causes, such as poverty, structural racism, and mental health issues. Addressing those issues could help to reduce it. Comprehensive gun laws are one piece of the puzzle of stopping gun violence.

A crime scene in Chicago, Illinois, in 2016. Chicago and other US cities experienced increased gun violence in 2019 and 2020.

CHAPTER 3
SOCIETY AND VIOLENCE

SYSTEMIC RACISM RESULTS IN MANY BLACK AND BROWN NEIGHBORHOODS FACING ECONOMIC INEQUITIES AND HAVING FEWER RESOURCES. Fewer resources mean fewer educational and career opportunities. These disadvantaged neighborhoods are especially impacted by gun violence. Gun violence is the leading cause of death for Black males younger than fifty-five. It is the second-leading cause for Latino males under thirty-four.

Struggling communities combined with easy access to guns means that violence can spark quickly. Beginning in 2019, many major cities saw new increases in gun violence. Even in states with strict gun laws, firearms can come in from neighboring states.

"This should be a wake-up call. We've been pressing the snooze button on this issue for too long and we're at the point where we can't press it anymore," said Chicago pastor Donovan Price.

Many instances of gun violence also have a tie to domestic violence. As of 2019, nearly one million women have reported being shot by an intimate partner. Every month more than fifty women are killed by a domestic partner. Women of color are affected by gun violence at a higher rate. Abusers use guns to control their partners through the threat of violence. And the effects of domestic violence can hurt children, family members, and friends, even if they are not an abuser's target.

Guns confiscated by the New York City Police Department

> "It's too easy to get a gun. Somebody intent on getting a gun is going to get one. We have to address public safety in our community in a few different ways."

—Muriel Bowser, Washington, DC, mayor

Another alarming piece of America's gun violence problem is white supremacist beliefs. Terror attacks in the US commonly take the form of mass shootings. In 2018 white supremacists were behind 78 percent of extremist-caused deaths.

Police officers and FBI agents arrive at the scene of the Tree of Life synagogue shooting in 2018. A gunman opened fire on Jewish people worshipping at the synagogue in Pittsburgh, Pennsylvania.

Moms Demand Action advocates against gun violence in the US.

CHAPTER 4
A SAFER AMERICA

THE PROBLEM OF GUN VIOLENCE CAN FEEL OVERWHELMING. But many organizations and lawmakers are working to slow the violence.

Commonsense gun reform is aimed at closing loopholes in current laws. For example, one reform would make it harder for known domestic abusers to get guns. Organizations such as Brady: United Against Gun Violence and the Coalition to Stop Gun Violence also want to pass new laws. An example is laws requiring universal background checks on all gun purchases. Bans on long assault rifles and high-capacity magazines can also play a part in reducing mass shootings.

First Lady Laura Bush meets with members of CeaseFire, an anti-violence organization in Chicago, in 2005.

Much of the focus on gun reform is at the national level. But local and state governments can help in slowing gun violence too. Some nonprofits work with cities to treat gun violence not as a crime problem but as a health issue. Programs such as Cure Violence use violence interrupters to hear disputes between individuals to try to prevent violence. In Chicago, the program's CeaseFire branch directly reduced shootings by an average of 42 percent in certain neighborhoods.

SMART GUN TECH

Researchers are developing ways to make guns safer. This could help to reduce violence. Smart gun technology requires fingerprints or radio frequency identification signals to make the weapon work. This could cut down on illegal acquisitions or thefts of guns. Microstamping leaves tiny identifying marks on a cartridge when a gun is fired, making it easier to trace the weapon.

Gun manufacturer Smith & Wesson presented this smart gun prototype in 2000. It uses technology to prohibit anyone but the gun's owner from firing it.

REFLECT

What laws do you think should be passed to help end gun violence?

An idea that gained popularity in 2020 is to reduce police funding. Instead of cities spending more money on police weaponry or vehicles, funding could go to programs and first responders that prevent violence.

Police department budgets are often far higher than those for social services that could help to curb gun violence.

In December 2019, marchers protested gun violence outside the Supreme Court Building in Washington, DC.

About 60 percent of Americans say they want stricter gun laws. But guns and gun violence are tied into larger issues. It will take reform in many parts of society to end the problem of gun violence in the US.

TAKE ACTION

Here are some ideas to help stop gun violence. What other ways could you help end gun violence?

Research gun violence as a public health issue at https://efsgv.org.

Join a local or neighborhood group dedicated to stopping gun violence.

Check out the Wear Orange movement at https://wearorange.org.

Contact your local or state representatives to ask what they are doing to prevent gun violence.

Learn more about the issue of gun violence in the US. Check out the Read Woke Reading List on page 30.

TIMELINE

1791: The Second Amendment becomes law, giving Americans the right to bear arms.

1934: The National Firearms Act is passed. It taxes people and businesses making and selling or buying shotguns and rifles to try to reduce gun violence. The act also creates a national registry of certain firearms.

1939: The Supreme Court rules that the Second Amendment does not guarantee the right to carry a sawed-off shotgun.

1968: President Lyndon Johnson signs the Gun Control Act. It bans the sale of guns to certain groups such as minors, people convicted of felonies, and others.

1994–2004: A national ban on assault weapons made it illegal to make or use high-powered firearms for civilian use.

2008: The Supreme Court rules that an individual has the right to keep a firearm at home independent of service in a state militia.

2013: Hadiya Pendleton is killed one week after performing at Obama's inaugural parade. Her family and friends launch the Wear Orange movement to raise awareness about gun violence.

2017: The US records 39,773 gun-related deaths, the most since 1968.

2018: The March for Our Lives draws two hundred thousand people to Washington, DC, to call for stricter gun laws.

2020: The US records 42,042 gun-related deaths as of December 21.

GLOSSARY

acquisition: buying or receiving something

arsenal: a collection of weapons

automatic: a type of firearm that fires repeatedly until the trigger is released

cartridge: a container holding propellant and a bullet in a gun

chapter: a local branch of a club or organization

extremist: someone who has extreme political or religious beliefs

inequity: lack of fairness or justice

lobby: to try to influence public officials, particularly legislators

loophole: a small exception or oversight in a law

magazine: the container holding cartridges in a gun

militia: an armed group called to serve as soldiers only in emergencies

patriotism: the love and pride people feel in their country

semiautomatic: a type of firearm operated partly automatically and partly by hand

SOURCE NOTES

5   Kelly Bauer, "Why Do People Wear Orange to Promote Gun Control? It All Started with Hadiya Pendleton," Block Club Chicago, June 7, 2019, https://blockclubchicago.org/2019/06 /07/why-do-people-wear-orange-to-promote-gun-control -it-all-started-with-hadiya-pendleton/.

5   Evelyn Holmes, "Community Marks Hadiya Pendleton's Birthday with Wear Orange Party for Peace," *ABC 7 Eyewitness News*, June 2, 2018, https://abc7chicago.com/hadiya-pendleton -wear-orange-gun-violence-awareness/3552119/.

6   Michael D. Shear, "Students Lead Huge Rallies for Gun Control across the U.S.," *New York Times*, March 24, 2018, https://www .nytimes.com/2018/03/24/us/politics/students-lead-huge -rallies-for-gun-control-across-the-us.html.

10   Josiah Bates, "'We Are Not Helpless Here,' Obama Responds to Mass Shootings in Dayton, El Paso," *Time*, August 5, 2019, https://time.com/5644593/obama-statement-mass-shootings -texas-dayton/.

14   Russell Berman, "Where the Gun-Control Movement Goes Silent," *Atlantic*, March 1, 2018, https://www.theatlantic.com /politics/archive/2018/03/guns-second-amendment-repeal /554540/.

17   Josiah Bates, "'We Should Have a Handle on This by Now.' As Inner-City Neighborhoods See a Surge in Gun Violence, These Are the Changes Community Leaders Say They Need," *Time*, July 27, 2020, https://time.com/5757773/inner-city-gun -violence/.

18   Bates.

READ WOKE READING LIST

Braun, Eric. *Never Again: The Parkland Shooting and the Teen Activists Leading a Movement*. Minneapolis: Lerner Publications, 2019.

Kiddle: Second Amendment Facts for Kids
https://kids.kiddle.co/Second_Amendment_to_the_United_States_Constitution

Louis, David Levering. *The Right to Bear Arms: A Look at the Second Amendment.* New York: PowerKids, 2019.

Mulford, Zoe. *The President Sang Amazing Grace*. Petaluma, CA: Cameron Kids, 2019.

Rhodes, Jewell Parker. *Ghost Boys*. New York: Little, Brown, 2018.

Second Amendment Facts for Kids
https://www.coolkidfacts.com/second-amendment-facts/

Students Demand Action
https://studentsdemandaction.org

Waters, Michael W. *For Beautiful Black Boys Who Believe in a Better World*. Louisville: Flyaway Books, 2020.

INDEX

background check, 19
ban, 9, 19

cause, 15–16, 18

law, 6, 10, 14–15, 17, 19, 22–23

March for Our Lives, 6
mass shooting, 10, 18–19

National Rifle Association, 13

reform, 6, 19–20, 23
right, 11–13

Second Amendment, 11–15
Supreme Court, 13

Wear Orange, 4–5

PHOTO ACKNOWLEDGMENTS

Image credits: lev radin/Shutterstock.com, pp. 4, 5; Taylor McKnight/Shutterstock.com, p. 6; Lutsenko_Oleksandr/Shutterstock.com, p. 7; Julia Fellers/Shutterstock.com, p. 8; Nicole Glass Photography/Shutterstock.com, p. 9; Evan Vucci/Photographer, p. 10; Chuck Jines/Shutterstock.com, p. 11; RonBailey/Getty Images, p. 12; REUTERS/Alamy Stock Photo, p. 13; Pamela Au/Shutterstock.com, p. 14; Ron Adar/Shutterstock.com, p. 15; AP Photo/M. Spencer Green, p. 16; Richard Levine/Alamy Stock Photo, p. 17; Brendt A Petersen/Shutterstock.com, p. 18; Phil Pasquini/Shutterstock.com, p. 19; AP Photo/Charles Rex Arbogast, p. 20; Porter Gifford/Liaison/Getty Images, p. 21; AP Photo/Mark Lennihan, p. 22; Rena Schild/Shutterstock.com, p. 23 Cecily Lewis portrait photos by Fernando Decillis.

Design elements: Ajay Shrivastava/Shutterstock.com; Milano Art/Shutterstock.com.

Cover image: nexusby/Shutterstock.com.

Content consultant: Lauren Footman, Director of Outreach and Equity, Educational Fund to Stop Gun Violence, Coalition to Stop Gun Violence

Lerner Publications Company
An imprint of Lerner Publishing Group, Inc.
241 First Avenue North
Minneapolis, MN 55401 USA

For reading levels and more information, look up this title at www.lernerbooks.com.

Main body text set in Aptifer Sans LT Pro.
Typeface provided by Linotype AG.

Library of Congress Cataloging-in-Publication Data

Names: Smith, Elliott, 1976– author.
Title: Gun violence and the fight for public safety / Elliott Smith.
Description: Minneapolis : Lerner Publications, 2022 | Series: Issues in action (Read Woke Books) | Includes bibliographical references and index. | Audience: Ages 9–14 | Audience: Grades 4–6 | Summary: "Gun violence has had a continued impact on public safety. This title takes a closer look at the effects of gun violence on specific demographics and American society"— Provided by publisher.
Identifiers: LCCN 2020052401 (print) | LCCN 2020052402 (ebook) | ISBN 9781728423401 (library binding) | ISBN 9781728431345 (paperback) | ISBN 9781728430669 (ebook)
Subjects: LCSH: Gun control—United States—Juvenile literature. | Firearms ownership—United States—Juvenile literature. | Violence—United States—Juvenile literature.
Classification: LCC HV7436 .S595 2022 (print) | LCC HV7436 (ebook) | DDC 363.330973—dc23

LC record available at https://lccn.loc.gov/2020052401
LC ebook record available at https://lccn.loc.gov/2020052402

Manufactured in the United States of America
1-49178-49309-3/22/2021